Music Minus One Vocals

NIGHT CLUB STANDARDS

Vol. 1 - Female

2131

Music Minus One
50 Executive Boulevard • Elmsford, New York 10523-1325
914-592-1188 • e-mail: info@musicminusone.com
www.musicminusone.com

Night Club Standards

Vol. 1 - Female

CONTENTS

ISBN 978-1-941566-31-2

MMO 2131

The More I See You

from the Twentieth Century-Fox Technicolor Music
BILLY ROSE'S DIAMOND HORSESHOE

Words by Mack Gordon
Music by Harry Warren

It Had To Be You

Words by Gus Kahn
Music by Isham Jones

The Shadow of Your Smile

Love Theme from THE SANDPIPER

Lyrics by Paul Francis Webster
Music by Johnny Mandel

MMO 2131

Watch What Happens
from THE UMBRELLAS OF CHERBOURG

Words by Gus Kahn
Music by Isham JonesMusic by Michel Legrand
Original French Text by Jacques Demy
English Lyrics by Norman Gimbel

The Good Life

Words by Jack Reardon
Music by Sacha DISTEL

Call Me Irresponsible

from the Paramount Picture PAPA'S DELICATE CONDITION

Words by Sammy Cahn
Music by James Van Heusen

Street Of Dreams

Words and Music by
Sam Lewis and Victor Young

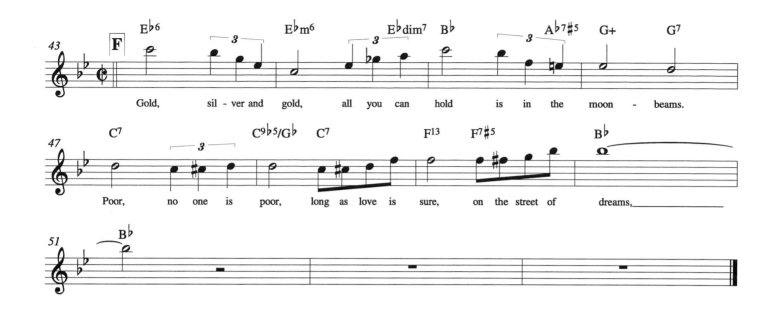

Gold, sil - ver and gold, all you can hold is in the moon - beams.

Poor, no one is poor, long as love is sure, on the street of dreams,____

I Should Care

Words by Sammy Cahn and Paul Weston
Music by Alex Stordahl and Paul Weston

I should care, I should go a - round

weep - in', I should care, I should go with - out

sleep - in' Strange - ly e - nough, I sleep well, 'cept for a dream or

two But then, I count my sheep well, Fun - ny how sheep can

lull you to sleep, So I should care, I should let it up -

Music Minus One
50 Executive Boulevard • Elmsford, New York 10523-1325
914-592-1188 • e-mail: info@musicminusone.com
www.musicminusone.com

MMO 2131

ISBN 978-1-941566-31-2